STOP WASTING AD MO
27 PROVEN HACKS TO SKYROCKE
MEDIA ENGAGEMENT IN THIRTY DAYS

WRITTEN BY JEFF SCOFFIELD

Chapter	Chapter

Introduction: Stop Wasting Ad Money and Skyrocket Engagement!

Are you tired of pouring money into social media ads that seem to disappear into a black hole? You're not alone. Countless businesses struggle to see a return on their investment when it comes to social media marketing.

This book is your escape hatch from the frustrating cycle of ineffective ads and low engagement. We'll equip you with 27 proven hacks you can implement in just 30 days to completely transform your social media presence.

Here's what you'll discover:

- Why your current ads aren't working (and how to fix them fast)
- The secret to crafting content that captivates your audience and compels them to engage
- Powerful strategies to spark conversations, build communities, and turn followers into loyal customers
- How to target your ideal audience with laser precision and maximize your return on ad spend

Forget wasting another dime on ineffective campaigns. This book is your roadmap to unlocking the true power of social media and finally achieving the engagement you deserve.

This introduction sets the stage by highlighting the reader's pain point (wasting ad money) and promises a solution (27 hacks for skyrocketing engagement). It also emphasizes the timeframe (30 days) to create a sense of urgency.

Chapter 1: Is Your Content Invisible? Identifying Weaknesses in Your Social Strategy

Have you ever poured your heart and soul into a social media post, only to see it get crickets in response? It's a frustrating feeling, and it happens to the best of us. The truth is, creating content isn't enough. You need to be crafting content that cuts through the noise and grabs your audience's attention.

This chapter is your detective kit for uncovering the reasons why your content might be getting lost in the social media shuffle. We'll identify the key weaknesses in your strategy and equip you with the tools to make your content stand out.

The Invisibility Culprits:

Here are some of the most common reasons why your content might be failing to resonate with your audience:

- **Bland and Boring:** Is your content generic or repetitive? Does it lack a unique voice or perspective? People crave authenticity and fresh ideas. We'll explore strategies to inject personality and spark interest in your content.
- **Misaligned Messaging:** Are you talking at your audience instead of with them? Does your

content address their needs and pain points? We'll help you refine your messaging to ensure it resonates with your target audience.

- **Content Quality Conundrum:** Is your content poorly written, riddled with typos, or visually unappealing? First impressions matter, and low-quality content can instantly turn people off. We'll provide tips on crafting high-quality content that reflects professionalism and care.
- **Inconsistent Posting:** Are you a social media ghost who appears sporadically? Consistency is key to building a loyal following. We'll develop strategies for establishing a consistent posting schedule that keeps your audience engaged.
- **Feature Fear:** Are you neglecting the built-in features of each platform? Platforms like Instagram Stories and live video offer incredible engagement opportunities. We'll explore various features and teach you how to leverage them effectively.

The Invisibility Cure:

By identifying the weaknesses in your strategy, you can take targeted action to improve your content's visibility and engagement. Here's what you'll gain from this chapter:

- A checklist to assess your current content strategy
- Tips for crafting content that resonates with your audience
- Strategies for maintaining consistency and leveraging platform features

Remember, invisibility is the enemy of engagement. This chapter equips you with the tools to diagnose your content's weaknesses and create posts that shine in the social media spotlight.

Chapter 2: Audience AWOL? Understanding Who You're Talking To (and Why They're Not Listening)

Ever feel like you're shouting into the social media void? You're crafting fantastic content, but your target audience seems to be missing in action. The culprit? A disconnect between who you're talking to and who you're actually reaching.

This chapter is your guide to truly understanding your ideal audience. By getting inside their heads (in a good way!), you can tailor your content to resonate with their needs and interests, ultimately turning them into engaged followers.

The Audience AWOL Mystery:

Here's why your target audience might not be showing up:

- **Demographic Delusion:** Are you basing your content on assumptions rather than concrete data? Demographics like age, location, and income can paint a picture of your ideal customer. We'll show you how to utilize social media analytics and audience research tools to gain a clear understanding of who you're trying to reach.

- **Interest Intrigue:** What keeps your audience up at night (figuratively speaking)? What are their passions, challenges, and aspirations? Understanding their interests allows you to create content that directly addresses their needs and desires. We'll provide strategies for uncovering your audience's interests and tailoring your content accordingly.
- **The Wrong Watering Hole:** Are you trying to attract dolphins on a mountaintop? Different social media platforms cater to different demographics and interests. Choosing the right platforms is crucial for reaching your target audience. We'll help you identify the platforms where your ideal audience spends their time online.
- **Language Lapse:** Are you speaking a foreign language to your audience? Tailoring your communication style and tone to resonate with your audience is key. We'll provide tips on using the right language and avoiding jargon that might alienate your followers.

The Audience Attraction Formula:

By understanding your audience, you can craft content that acts like a magnet, attracting and engaging them. Here's what you'll gain from this chapter:

- Techniques to define your ideal customer persona
- Strategies to identify your target audience's demographics and interests
- Guidance on selecting the most effective social media platforms for reaching your audience
- Tips on adapting your communication style to resonate with your followers

Remember, social media is a two-way street. By understanding your audience, you can create content that speaks directly to them, fostering meaningful connections and boosting engagement.

Chapter 3: The Engagement Killers: Spotting Common Mistakes Sabotaging Your Reach

You've created stellar content, you know your audience inside and out, but those likes and comments are still scarce. What gives? Sometimes, it's the subtle mistakes that can act like silent assassins, sabotaging your reach and engagement.

This chapter equips you with the eagle eye to spot these engagement killers lurking in your social media strategy. By identifying and eliminating these mistakes, you can watch your engagement soar.

The Silent Sabotage Squad:

Here are some common social media mistakes that might be hindering your reach:

- **The Visual Void:** In a world bombarded with content, visuals are king. Are your posts lacking eye-catching images, infographics, or videos? We'll explore the importance of visuals and provide tips on creating high-quality content that stops the scroll.
- **The Hashtag Hijack:** Hashtags can be a powerful tool for discovery, but using irrelevant or overly generic ones can hurt your reach. Are you using the right hashtags? We'll teach you how to research and implement effective hashtags to get your content seen by the right audience.
- **The Caption Catastrophe:** Are your captions long-winded snoozefests? Compelling captions can spark conversation and encourage engagement. We'll provide tips on crafting concise, attention-grabbing captions that entice people to read more and interact with your content.
- **The Ghost Poster:** Do you post once a month and then disappear into the social media ether? Consistency is key to building a loyal following. We'll develop strategies for creating a

consistent posting schedule that keeps your audience engaged.

- **The One-Way Conversation:** Social media is a dialogue, not a monologue. Are you responding to comments and messages? We'll show you the importance of social listening and interacting with your audience to foster a sense of community.
- **The Call to Action Conundrum:** Are you telling your audience what you want them to do after reading your post? Clear calls to action can significantly boost engagement. We'll provide tips on crafting compelling calls to action that encourage likes, comments, shares, and clicks.

Eradicating the Engagement Killers:

By identifying these common mistakes, you can take action to optimize your social media presence. Here's what you'll gain from this chapter:

- Strategies for creating visually appealing content
- Guidance on researching and using effective hashtags
- Tips for crafting compelling captions that drive engagement

- A plan for establishing a consistent posting schedule
- Techniques for fostering a two-way conversation with your audience
- Methods for incorporating clear calls to action in your content

Remember, small tweaks can make a big difference. By eliminating these engagement killers, you can unlock the full potential of your social media reach and watch your interactions skyrocket.

Chapter 4: The Science of Sharing: What Makes People Hit Like and Retweet

Ever wondered what makes people stop scrolling and engage with a particular social media post? The answer lies in understanding the psychology behind sharing. This chapter dives into the science of social influence and reveals the triggers that compel people to like, share, and comment on your content.

The Like Lab:

Here, we'll explore the key factors that influence people to hit like:

- **The Emotion Equation:** People are more likely to engage with content that evokes emotions. We'll delve into the power of humor, inspiration, and storytelling to trigger emotional responses and encourage likes.
- **The Reciprocity Rule:** People subconsciously feel obligated to return favors. By acknowledging their comments and responding to questions, you foster a sense of reciprocity, making them more likely to like your content in return.
- **The Bandwagon Effect:** People tend to follow the crowd. Highlighting positive reactions like existing likes and comments can create a

bandwagon effect, encouraging others to like as well.

- **The Recognition Reward:** Feeling acknowledged is a basic human desire. Tagging relevant people in your posts or mentioning them in replies gives them recognition and increases the likelihood of them liking your content.

The Retweet Revolution:

While likes are great, retweets are a whole new level of engagement. Here's what makes people retweet:

- **The Valuable Verdict:** People share content they perceive as valuable to their followers. We'll explore strategies for creating informative, educational, or entertaining content that your audience feels compelled to share.
- **The Credibility Catalyst:** People are more likely to share content from credible sources. Establishing yourself as an expert in your industry by sharing valuable insights builds trust and encourages retweets.
- **The Conversation Catalyst:** People share content that sparks conversations. Pose questions, host discussions, or share thought-provoking content to get people talking and retweeting to share their own perspectives.

- **The Trendsetter Tribe:** People want to be seen as "in the know." Identify trending topics or hashtags and incorporate them into your content strategically to tap into the trendsetter mentality and encourage retweets.

The Sharing Symphony:

By understanding these psychological triggers, you can compose content that resonates with your audience and compels them to like and share it. Here's what you'll gain from this chapter:

- Techniques to evoke emotions and encourage engagement
- Strategies for building reciprocity and fostering a community
- Tips for leveraging the bandwagon effect for increased likes
- Methods for creating valuable content that gets retweeted
- Techniques for establishing credibility and building trust
- Strategies for sparking conversations and encouraging discussion
- Tips for identifying and leveraging trending topics to boost retweets

Remember, social media is a social experience. By understanding the science of sharing, you can craft content that ignites engagement and positions you as a thought leader within your industry.

Chapter 5: Know Your Platform: Tailoring Content for Each Social Media Channel

The social media landscape is vast, with each platform catering to different audiences and content formats. A one-size-fits-all approach won't cut it. This chapter equips you with the knowledge to tailor your content for each platform, maximizing your reach and engagement.

The Platform Playground:

Here, we'll explore the unique characteristics of some of the most popular social media platforms:

- **Facebook:** The granddaddy of social media, Facebook boasts a diverse user base. Long-form content, including articles, infographics, and live videos, can perform well here, alongside engaging text posts and image shares.
- **Instagram:** The land of the visually stunning, Instagram thrives on high-quality photos, short videos (Reels), and captivating Stories. User-generated content (UGC) and influencer marketing also hold significant power on this platform.
- **Twitter:** Known for its fast-paced nature and breaking news, Twitter is ideal for concise, attention-grabbing posts with relevant hashtags.

Polls, live Q&A sessions, and witty tweets can also generate engagement.

- **LinkedIn:** The professional hub, LinkedIn caters to a more B2B (business-to-business) audience. Industry insights, thought leadership articles, and professional networking opportunities are key on this platform.
- **YouTube:** The video giant, YouTube offers immense potential for brand storytelling, educational content, product demonstrations, and engaging vlogs.

The Tailoring Toolbox:

Understanding how to adapt your content for each platform is crucial for success. Here's what you'll learn in this chapter:

- **Content format preferences:** Discover the ideal content formats (text, images, videos) for each platform to maximize reach.
- **Character count constraints:** Familiarize yourself with character limits for captions and posts on different platforms to avoid getting cut off.
- **Visual storytelling strategies:** Learn how to leverage visuals effectively on platforms like Instagram and Pinterest to capture attention.

- **Engagement features finesse:** Explore the unique engagement features of each platform (e.g., polls on Twitter, Stories on Instagram) to boost interaction.
- **Hashtag havens:** Identify the power of hashtags on different platforms and learn how to use them strategically for discovery.

The Platform Powerhouse:

By tailoring your content for each platform, you can become a social media powerhouse. This chapter equips you with the knowledge to:

- Craft content that resonates with specific audiences on each platform.
- Leverage platform-specific features to maximize engagement.
- Develop a diversified content calendar catering to different social media channels.

Remember, mastering the art of platform tailoring allows you to speak the language of each social media community, fostering deeper connections and achieving greater impact.

Chapter 6: Headline Havoc: Mastering the Art of Titles that Grab Attention

In the crowded world of social media, headlines are the battle cry that cuts through the noise and compels people to stop scrolling. A weak headline is like a whisper in a hurricane – easily lost and forgotten. This chapter equips you with the skills to craft magnetic headlines that grab attention, spark curiosity, and entice people to dive deeper into your content.

The Headline Hierarchy:

Headlines serve two crucial purposes:

- **Attention Magnet:** They act as a magnet, drawing people in and stopping them mid-scroll.
- **Content Compass:** They accurately reflect the content of your post, giving readers a clear idea of what to expect.

Headline Havoc Culprits:

Here are some common headline mistakes that can wreak havoc on your engagement:

- **The Bland and Boring Brigade:** Generic headlines like "5 Tips for..." or "Our Latest Blog Post" fail to stand out. We'll explore strategies to inject intrigue and personality into your headlines.

- **Clickbait Catastrophe:** Overly sensational headlines that don't deliver on their promises damage trust and credibility. We'll teach you to craft honest and informative headlines that still pique interest.
- **The Mystery Monster:** Headlines that are too vague leave readers guessing about the content. We'll provide tips on creating clear and concise headlines that accurately represent your post.

Headline Harmony Heroes:

By mastering the art of crafting captivating headlines, you can turn "headline havoc" into "headline harmony." Here's what you'll gain from this chapter:

- **Power words and phrases:** Discover a treasure trove of powerful words and phrases that trigger curiosity and compel clicks.
- **Number magic:** Learn how to effectively incorporate numbers into your headlines to grab attention and structure content.
- **Benefit-driven approach:** Craft headlines that highlight the benefits your content offers, enticing readers to learn more.

- **The question technique:** Pose thought-provoking questions in your headlines to spark curiosity and encourage engagement.
- **A/B testing tactics:** Explore the power of A/B testing different headlines to see which ones resonate best with your audience.

The Headline Hero:

By implementing the strategies outlined in this chapter, you'll transform yourself from a headline novice to a headline hero. You'll be able to craft magnetic titles that act like irresistible invitations, pulling readers into your social media content and skyrocketing your engagement.

Chapter 7: Content Calendar Chaos? Planning and Scheduling for Consistent Engagement

Feeling overwhelmed by the constant pressure to churn out fresh social media content? You're not alone. Many businesses struggle to maintain a consistent posting schedule, leading to content calendar chaos and ultimately, dwindling engagement.

This chapter is your roadmap to conquering the content calendar beast. We'll equip you with strategies for planning, scheduling, and streamlining your social media content creation process, ensuring a steady flow of high-quality content that keeps your audience engaged.

The Content Calendar Conundrum:

Here's why content calendar chaos happens:

- **Planning Paralysis:** Feeling overwhelmed by the sheer volume of content needed can lead to procrastination and missed deadlines.
- **Inspiration Impasse:** Hitting a wall of creative block can make it difficult to come up with fresh content ideas consistently.
- **Scheduling Scramble:** Manually scheduling posts across multiple platforms can be time-consuming and inefficient.

Conquering the Content Calendar:

By implementing these strategies, you can transform your content calendar from a source of stress to a well-oiled engagement machine:

- **Batching Bonanza:** Discover the power of batching your content creation process. Dedicate specific blocks of time to brainstorm ideas, capture photos and videos, and write captions for multiple posts.
- **Ideation Inspiration:** Explore strategies for generating a steady stream of content ideas. Utilize tools like content calendars with built-in suggestion features, leverage trending topics, and repurpose existing content into new formats.
- **The Power of Planning:** Develop a content calendar template that outlines your posting schedule for different platforms. Allocate specific days and times for each type of content (e.g., Mondays for industry insights, Wednesdays for inspirational quotes).
- **Scheduling Savvy:** Utilize social media scheduling tools to automate the process of publishing your content across multiple platforms, saving you valuable time and ensuring consistency.

- **Content Curation Collaboration:** Don't be afraid to curate high-quality content from credible sources and share it with your audience. This can supplement your original content and provide valuable insights to your followers.

The Content Calendar Champion:

By mastering these strategies, you'll transition from a content calendar casualty to a champion. You'll be able to:

- Develop a streamlined and efficient content creation process.
- Generate a consistent flow of fresh and engaging content.
- Save valuable time and resources by utilizing scheduling tools.
- Maintain a strong brand voice and presence across all social media platforms.

Remember, consistency is key to building a loyal following and nurturing long-term engagement. This chapter equips you with the tools and strategies to conquer content calendar chaos and establish a content creation process that fuels your social media success.

Chapter 8: Beyond the Text: Using Visuals to Stop the Scroll (and Spark Conversation)

In today's fast-paced social media landscape, attention spans are shorter than ever. Text-heavy posts often get lost in the never-ending scroll. This chapter dives into the power of visuals and equips you with strategies to create captivating content that grabs attention, sparks conversation, and ultimately, boosts engagement.

The Visual Advantage:

Visuals are the silent language of social media. Here's why they hold immense power:

- **Attention Magnets:** High-quality images, infographics, and videos instantly capture attention and stop the scroll in its tracks.
- **Emotional Triggers:** Visuals can evoke powerful emotions, creating a deeper connection with your audience and making your content more memorable.
- **Information Simplification:** Complex ideas can be communicated more effectively and efficiently through compelling visuals.
- **Storytelling Powerhouse:** Pictures truly are worth a thousand words. Visuals allow you to tell engaging stories that resonate with your audience on a deeper level.

Beyond Stock Photos:

While stock photos can be a helpful starting point, there's a whole world of visual storytelling options to explore. Here are some creative ideas:

- **Original Photography:** Showcase your brand personality and capture unique moments with high-quality product or lifestyle photos.
- **Eye-Catching Graphics:** Utilize design tools to create infographics, charts, or illustrations that present data and information in a visually appealing way.
- **Behind-the-Scenes Glimpses:** Give your audience a peek into your company culture and team with authentic behind-the-scenes photos and videos.
- **User-Generated Content (UGC) Magic:** Encourage your audience to share their own photos and videos related to your brand, fostering a sense of community and authenticity.
- **Humor in Action:** Don't be afraid to inject some humor into your visuals with funny memes, GIFs, or illustrations. (Remember to tailor humor to your brand and audience.)

Visuals that Spark Conversation:

Simply posting a pretty picture isn't enough. Here's how to use visuals to spark conversation and boost engagement:

- **Pose Engaging Questions:** Overlay thought-provoking questions on your visuals to encourage your audience to share their opinions and spark discussions.
- **Run Contests and Giveaways:** Host contests or giveaways that require participants to share photos or videos related to your brand, increasing user-generated content and engagement.
- **Polls and Quizzes:** Utilize visual elements like polls and quizzes to gather audience insights and spark conversations around trending topics in your industry.
- **Live Video Broadcasts:** Host live video sessions where you can interact with your audience in real-time, showcasing your expertise and fostering a sense of connection.

The Visual Storytelling Champion:

By mastering the art of visual storytelling, you can transform your social media presence. Here's what you'll gain from this chapter:

- Techniques for creating high-quality and engaging visuals

- Strategies for leveraging different visual content formats
- Tips for incorporating user-generated content into your social media strategy
- Methods for using visuals to spark conversation and encourage interaction
- Ideas for incorporating humor and personality into your visual content

Remember, visuals are a powerful tool for cutting through the noise and connecting with your audience on a deeper level. This chapter equips you to become a visual storytelling champion, creating content that stops the scroll, sparks conversations, and propels your social media engagement to new heights.

Chapter 9: The Power of the Question: Sparking Discussions and Building Relationships

In the social media age, where content saturation reigns supreme, simply broadcasting information isn't enough. To truly engage your audience and build a loyal following, you need to foster two-way communication. This chapter explores the power of the question – a simple yet effective tool for sparking discussions, building relationships, and skyrocketing your social media engagement.

The Question Conundrum:

Many businesses shy away from asking questions on social media, fearing they might appear unsure or lacking expertise. However, the opposite is true. Here's why questions are a secret weapon for social media success:

- **Engagement Engine:** Questions instantly break the ice and invite your audience to participate in the conversation. This two-way interaction fosters a sense of community and keeps people coming back for more.
- **Audience Insights Arsenal:** By asking thoughtful questions, you gain valuable insights into your audience's needs, wants, and pain points. This information can be used to tailor

your content strategy and better serve your followers.

- **Relationship Builder:** When you ask questions, you demonstrate genuine interest in your audience. This fosters trust and builds stronger relationships with your followers.
- **Content Inspiration Powerhouse:** Struggling for content ideas? Questions can be a springboard for brainstorming engaging topics and sparking creative discussions.

The Art of Asking:

Not all questions are created equal. Here's how to craft questions that ignite conversation and boost engagement:

- **Open-Ended Odyssey:** Move beyond yes-or-no questions. Opt for open-ended questions that encourage elaborate responses and spark discussions. (e.g., "What's your biggest challenge when it comes to...?" or "What content would you love to see more of from us?")
- **Thought-Provoking Inquiries:** Pose questions that challenge assumptions and encourage critical thinking. This type of intellectual engagement keeps your audience coming back

for more. (e.g., "If you could change one thing about your industry, what would it be?")

- **Personal Touch Magic:** Personalize your questions to specific followers or segments of your audience. This demonstrates that you care about their unique perspectives. (e.g., "Designers, what are your favorite tools for creating social media graphics?")
- **Trending Topic Tango:** Tap into current events and trending topics by asking questions related to your industry. This positions you as a thought leader and keeps your content relevant. (e.g., "What are your thoughts on the latest social media algorithm update?")

The Question Master:

By incorporating the power of the question into your social media strategy, you'll transform yourself from a one-way communicator to a conversation facilitator. Here's what you'll gain from this chapter:

- Techniques for crafting compelling and engaging questions
- Strategies for using questions to gather valuable audience insights
- Tips for fostering a sense of community through two-way communication

- Methods for leveraging questions to spark creative content ideas
- Ideas for incorporating trending topics and personalization into your questions

Remember, questions are the key to unlocking meaningful connections and building lasting relationships with your audience. Embrace the power of the question and watch your social media engagement soar.

Chapter 10: Contests and Giveaways: The Ultimate Traffic Booster

Who doesn't love a good giveaway? Contests and giveaways are powerful tools for attracting new followers, boosting brand awareness, and generating excitement around your social media presence. This chapter dives into the strategic use of contests and giveaways to supercharge your social media traffic and engagement.

The Traffic Tampering Tribulations:

Organic reach on social media platforms can be a struggle. Many businesses find it challenging to attract new followers and get their content seen by a wider audience. This is where contests and giveaways come in as potential saviors.

The Giveaway Glitz and Glamour:

Here's why contests and giveaways are so effective:

- **Attention Grabbers:** The allure of winning a free prize naturally grabs attention and entices people to participate. This can significantly increase visibility and attract new followers.
- **Engagement Explosion:** Contests that require participants to like, comment, or share your

posts can dramatically boost engagement metrics.

- **Brand Awareness Bonanza:** Giveaways associated with your brand or products increase brand awareness and recognition among a wider audience.
- **Lead Generation Magnet:** Contests can be a great way to collect valuable leads by requiring participants to submit their email addresses or follow your social media accounts.

The Giveaway Game Plan:

Not all contests are created equal. Here's how to design and implement effective contests and giveaways that deliver results:

- **Define Your Goals:** Clearly identify your objectives for the contest. Are you aiming to increase brand awareness, generate leads, or drive traffic to your website?
- **Pick the Perfect Prize:** Choose a prize that is relevant to your target audience and aligns with your brand identity. The prize should be enticing enough to encourage participation.
- **Craft Compelling Contest Mechanics:** Develop clear and easy-to-understand contest rules and entry guidelines.

- **Promote Your Giveaway Powerhouse:** Utilize various channels to promote your contest, including your social media platforms, email marketing campaigns, and influencer collaborations.
- **Announce the Winner with Flair:** Don't just announce the winner – celebrate them! Publicly announce the winner and showcase their participation, fostering goodwill and encouraging future engagement.

Beyond the Free Stuff:

While giveaways are attractive, remember to focus on building long-term relationships. Here's how to leverage contests for sustainable growth:

- **Nurture New Followers:** Don't let new followers gained through the contest simply vanish. Develop a strategy to nurture them into loyal fans by providing valuable content and ongoing engagement opportunities.
- **Offer Valuable Content Incentives:** Consider incorporating non-material prizes alongside giveaways. Offer exclusive content, consultations, or early access to new products as contest rewards.

- **Host Recurring Contests:** Regularly host contests to maintain momentum and excitement around your brand.

The Traffic Titan:

By strategically implementing contests and giveaways, you can transform yourself from a traffic struggler to a traffic titan. Here's what you'll gain from this chapter:

- Strategies for setting clear goals for your contests
- Tips for selecting the perfect prize to incentivize participation
- Techniques for crafting engaging contest mechanics and entry guidelines
- Methods for effectively promoting your contests across multiple channels
- Ideas for nurturing new followers and building long-term engagement

Remember, contests and giveaways can be a powerful tool for boosting your social media presence. However, true success lies in using them as a stepping stone to building a loyal community around your brand.

Chapter 11: Live Like a Pro: Leveraging Live Video to Connect with Your Audience

In today's social media landscape, authenticity and real-time connection are more valuable than ever. Live video streaming platforms offer a unique opportunity to break down the barriers between brands and audiences, fostering deeper connections and boosting engagement. This chapter equips you with the knowledge and strategies to become a live video pro, effectively using live streams to connect with your audience on a whole new level.

The Live Video Revolution:

Live video has exploded in popularity, offering several advantages over traditional pre-recorded content:

- **Unfiltered Authenticity:** Live video allows you to showcase the real, human side of your brand, fostering trust and connection with your audience.
- **Real-Time Engagement:** Live streams create a space for two-way interaction. You can answer questions in real-time, respond to comments, and build a sense of community.
- **Increased Visibility:** Many social media platforms prioritize live content in user feeds,

giving you the potential to reach a wider audience.

- **Memorable Moments:** Live streams create a sense of urgency and excitement, making them more likely to be remembered by viewers.

Conquering Your Live Video Fears:

The idea of going live can be daunting. Here are some common fears associated with live video and how to overcome them:

- **Technical Glitches:** While technical difficulties can happen, thorough preparation (testing your equipment and internet connection) and having a backup plan can minimize mishaps.
- **Going Blank:** Prepare talking points and have visuals on hand to avoid awkward silences. However, embrace the opportunity to be spontaneous and conversational.
- **Negative Comments:** Develop a thick skin and have a strategy for moderating comments to ensure a positive and respectful environment.

Live Streaming Like a Star:

Here's how to transform yourself from a live video novice to a live streaming star:

- **Captivating Content Concepts:** Plan engaging live streams that offer value to your audience. Host Q&A sessions, product demonstrations, behind-the-scenes tours, or live interviews with industry experts.
- **Promote Your Live Event:** Generate buzz for your live stream by promoting it across your social media platforms and email marketing campaigns. Create a sense of anticipation and encourage viewers to set reminders.
- **Be Yourself and Have Fun!** Relax, be yourself, and let your personality shine through. Your passion and enthusiasm will be contagious and draw viewers in.
- **Post-Live Engagement:** Don't let the interaction end after the live stream. Share a recording of the session, respond to comments, and answer lingering questions to maintain engagement.

The Live Video Link Builder:

By mastering the art of live video, you can become a live video link builder, creating stronger connections with your audience and fostering a thriving online community. Here's what you'll gain from this chapter:

- Strategies for overcoming common live video anxieties

- Tips for developing engaging live stream content concepts
- Techniques for effectively promoting your live streams and generating anticipation
- Methods for optimizing your live presentation style for maximum audience connection
- Ideas for extending engagement beyond the live stream

Remember, live video is a powerful tool for humanizing your brand and building genuine relationships with your audience. Embrace the immediacy and authenticity of live streams, and watch your social media presence transform.

Chapter 12: Stories Unleashed: Decoding the Power of Instagram and Facebook Stories

The world of social media is constantly evolving, and Stories have become a dominant force on platforms like Instagram and Facebook. These ephemeral snippets of content offer a unique space for sharing behind-the-scenes glimpses, fostering real-time interactions, and keeping your audience engaged. This chapter equips you with the knowledge to unlock the power of Stories, transforming you from a spectator to a master storyteller.

The Story Surge:

Stories have taken the social media world by storm for several reasons:

- **Ephemeral Excitement:** The disappearing nature of Stories (usually lasting 24 hours) creates a sense of urgency and excitement, encouraging viewers to tune in before they're gone.
- **Authenticity on Autopilot:** Stories allow you to share unfiltered, behind-the-scenes moments, giving your audience a peek into the real side of your brand.
- **Interactive Playground:** Stories come packed with interactive features like polls, quizzes, and

questions, fostering two-way communication and keeping your audience engaged.

- **Data-Driven Decisions:** Built-in analytics allow you to track vital metrics like completion rates and engagement on your Stories, providing valuable insights to optimize your content strategy.

Beyond the Boomerang:

Stories are more than just selfies and silly filters. Here are creative ideas for using Stories to captivate your audience:

- **Product Demos and Tutorials:** Showcase your products in action or offer step-by-step tutorials using Stories' features.
- **Behind-the-Scenes Access:** Give your audience a glimpse into your company culture, team members, or events through candid Stories.
- **Host Q&A Sessions:** Leverage the question sticker feature to host interactive Q&A sessions and address your audience's curiosities in real-time.
- **Story Takeovers:** Invite influencers, industry experts, or even customers to take over your Stories for a unique perspective and wider reach.

- **Live Polls and Quizzes:** Spark conversations and gather audience insights with interactive polls and quizzes incorporated into your Stories.

Storytelling Strategies:

Crafting compelling Stories requires a strategic approach. Here are some tips to maximize your impact:

- **Captivating Intros:** Hook viewers from the get-go with eye-catching visuals, intriguing questions, or attention-grabbing text.
- **Visual Storytelling:** Stories are a visual medium. Utilize high-quality photos, videos, and text overlays to keep your content engaging.
- **Story Arcs:** Think of your Stories as mini-narratives with a beginning, middle, and end. Use a logical sequence and CTAs (calls to action) to guide viewers through your content.
- **Post Consistently:** Maintain a consistent Stories posting schedule to keep your audience engaged and coming back for more.
- **Data-Driven Decisions:** Analyze your Stories insights to see what resonates with your audience and adapt your strategy accordingly.

The Story Sorcerer:

By mastering the art of Stories, you'll transform yourself from a Story spectator into a Story sorcerer. Here's what you'll gain from this chapter:

- Techniques for creating captivating and engaging Stories content
- Creative ideas for leveraging Stories features for maximum impact
- Strategies for incorporating audience interaction into your Stories
- Tips for analyzing Stories insights and optimizing your content
- Methods for developing a consistent Stories posting schedule

Remember, Stories are a powerful tool for humanizing your brand, fostering real-time connections, and keeping your audience glued to your social media presence. Unleash the power of Stories and watch your engagement soar.

Chapter 13: Building Communities: Fostering a Loyal Following Through Groups and Forums

In today's digital age, social media goes beyond just broadcasting messages. It's about creating a space for connection, fostering a sense of belonging, and cultivating a loyal following. This chapter delves into the power of online communities – groups and forums – as a tool for building lasting relationships with your audience and establishing yourself as a thought leader in your industry.

The Loneliness Factor:

Despite being constantly connected, many people crave a sense of community online. Social media groups and forums offer a platform for people with shared interests to connect, discuss topics, and support each other.

The Community Catalyst:

By creating or actively participating in relevant online communities, you can achieve several benefits:

- **Brand Advocacy:** Cultivate a community of brand advocates who organically promote your products or services through positive word-of-mouth within the group.

- **Valuable Customer Insights:** Gain valuable insights into your target audience's needs, wants, and pain points by listening to the conversations happening within the community.
- **Enhanced Brand Authority:** Establish yourself as a thought leader by providing valuable information, answering questions, and engaging in discussions within the community.
- **Customer Support Hub:** Offer a platform for your customers to connect with each other and get peer-to-peer support, reducing the burden on your own customer service team.

Cultivating Your Community Corner:

There are various types of online communities to consider, each with its own strengths:

- **Branded Groups:** Create a dedicated group on a platform like Facebook where you control the rules and can directly promote your brand and offerings.
- **Industry Forums:** Participate in established industry forums to connect with a wider audience and showcase your expertise.
- **Niche Social Networks:** Explore niche social networks catering to your specific industry or target audience.

Building a Thriving Community:

Here's how to nurture and grow a thriving online community:

- **Clearly Defined Purpose:** Establish a clear purpose and set of guidelines for your community. This ensures a focused discussion and attracts the right audience.
- **Valuable Content and Conversation:** Provide value to your community by sharing informative content, offering expert advice, and actively participating in discussions.
- **Encourage Two-Way Communication:** Don't just broadcast messages. Foster two-way communication by asking questions, responding to comments, and encouraging healthy debate within the group.
- **Recognize and Reward Engagement:** Acknowledge and appreciate active members by highlighting their contributions and rewarding their participation.
- **Moderate with Care:** While establishing guidelines is important, avoid being overly restrictive. Foster a sense of openness and respect within the community.

The Community Champion:

By following these strategies, you can transform yourself from a community outsider to a community champion. Here's what you'll gain from this chapter:

- Understanding of the benefits of building online communities
- Knowledge of different types of online communities and their functionalities
- Tips for establishing and nurturing a thriving online community
- Strategies for providing value and fostering engagement within the community
- Techniques for moderating discussions and maintaining a positive environment

Remember, building a loyal following goes beyond likes and comments. By fostering a thriving online community, you create a space for genuine connection, establish long-term relationships with your audience, and position yourself as a trusted leader in your industry.

Chapter 14: Targeting Titans: Mastering Audience Targeting for Laser-Focused Campaigns

In the age of information overload, social media success hinges on reaching the right people with the right message at the right time. This chapter equips you with the knowledge and strategies to become a targeting titan, mastering the art of audience targeting for laser-focused social media campaigns that resonate with your ideal audience and deliver maximum impact.

The Scatter Shot Struggle:

Many businesses make the mistake of blasting generic messages to a broad audience. This scattershot approach is not only ineffective but can also be expensive. Here's why targeted campaigns are crucial:

- **Relevance Reigns Supreme:** People are more likely to engage with content that is relevant to their interests and needs. Targeted campaigns ensure your message reaches the right audience, maximizing engagement.
- **Boosting the ROI:** By targeting your ideal audience, you get more bang for your buck. You'll see a higher return on investment (ROI) on your social media advertising spend.

- **Brand Awareness Bonanza:** Targeted campaigns allow you to reach a wider audience within your specific niche, increasing brand awareness and recognition among potential customers.

The Targeting Toolbox:

Most social media platforms offer a multitude of targeting options. Here's a look at some key targeting tools you can leverage:

- **Demographics:** Target users based on factors like age, gender, location, income, and education level.
- **Interests:** Reach people based on their hobbies, passions, and online behaviors.
- **Behaviors:** Target users based on their purchase history, website visits, or app usage.
- **Lookalike Audiences:** Utilize existing customer data to create a "lookalike audience" of users with similar characteristics.

Targeting Triumphs:

Here are some strategies to take your audience targeting to the next level:

- **Buyer Persona Power:** Develop detailed buyer personas that represent your ideal customers.

This will guide your targeting decisions and ensure your content resonates with the right audience.

- **Layered Targeting Magic:** Combine different targeting options to create highly specific audience segments for your campaigns. This allows you to deliver hyper-relevant messages that convert.
- **A/B Testing for Targeting Tweaks:** Don't be afraid to experiment with different targeting options. Utilize A/B testing to see which audience segments perform best and refine your campaigns for maximum impact.
- **Keep Your Targeting Dynamic:** As your audience and the social media landscape evolve, so should your targeting strategies. Regularly review and update your targeting parameters to ensure optimal campaign performance.

The Targeting Trailblazer:

By mastering the art of audience targeting, you'll transform yourself from a targeting novice to a targeting trailblazer. Here's what you'll gain from this chapter:

- Understanding of the importance of targeted social media campaigns

- Knowledge of various audience targeting options offered by social media platforms
- Strategies for developing buyer personas to guide your targeting decisions
- Tips for effectively combining different targeting options for maximum reach
- Techniques for A/B testing your targeting strategies and optimizing campaigns

Remember, targeted social media campaigns are the key to unlocking true engagement and achieving your social media goals. By mastering the art of targeting, you can ensure your message cuts through the noise, resonates with your ideal audience, and propels your social media presence to new heights.

Chapter 15: Ad Copywriting Alchemy: Crafting Compelling Ads that Convert

In the competitive world of social media advertising, your ad copy is the magic potion that transforms viewers into paying customers. This chapter equips you with the secrets of ad copywriting alchemy, guiding you in crafting compelling ad copy that grabs attention, sparks interest, and ultimately drives conversions.

The Bland Banner Blues:

Generic ad copy that blends into the background is the enemy of social media success. Here's why powerful ad copy is crucial:

- **Attention Alchemist:** A well-written ad instantly captures attention, stopping the scroll and piquing viewers' curiosity.
- **The Desire Distillery:** Compelling ad copy effectively communicates the value proposition of your product or service, igniting a desire to learn more.
- **Conversion Catalyst:** Powerful ad copy compels viewers to take action, whether it's visiting your website, downloading an ebook, or making a purchase.

From Text to Alchemy:

Transforming basic text into potent ad copy requires a specific blend of ingredients:

- **Headline Hero:** Craft a captivating headline that grabs attention and entices viewers to read further. Utilize strong verbs, power words, and a touch of intrigue.
- **Benefit Bonanza:** Highlight the key benefits your product or service offers. Focus on how it solves a problem or improves the viewer's life.
- **Storytelling Spark:** Weave a mini-story into your ad copy to connect with viewers on an emotional level. Make them laugh, think, or feel something.
- **Call to Action Clarity:** End your ad with a clear call to action (CTA) that tells viewers exactly what you want them to do next.

The Art of Persuasion:

Here are some persuasive writing techniques to elevate your ad copy:

- **Problem-Solution Powerhouse:** Identify a common pain point your target audience faces and position your product or service as the solution.
- **Social Proof Magic:** Leverage social proof elements like testimonials, reviews, or

influencer endorsements to build trust and credibility.

- **Scarcity and Urgency:** Create a sense of urgency by highlighting limited-time offers or limited quantities. This encourages viewers to take action before they miss out.
- **Emotional Connection:** Connect with your audience on an emotional level by using evocative language and imagery that resonates with their desires and aspirations.

The Ad Copy Alchemist:

By mastering the art of ad copywriting alchemy, you'll transform yourself from a copywriting novice to a conversion-driven alchemist. Here's what you'll gain from this chapter:

- Techniques for crafting captivating ad headlines that grab attention
- Strategies for highlighting the key benefits of your product or service
- Tips for incorporating storytelling elements into your ad copy for emotional impact
- Methods for crafting clear and compelling calls to action that drive conversions
- Knowledge of persuasive writing techniques to enhance your ad copy effectiveness

Remember, your ad copy is your most valuable tool in the social media advertising landscape. By wielding the power of ad copywriting alchemy, you can craft irresistible ads that convert viewers into loyal customers and fuel your social media success.

Chapter 16: Budget Bonanza: Optimizing Your Ad Spend for Maximum ROI

In the world of social media advertising, where every penny counts, budget optimization is key. This chapter equips you with the knowledge and strategies to become a budgeting bonanza, ensuring you get the most out of your ad spend and achieve maximum return on investment (ROI).

The Bidding Black Hole:

Uninformed budgeting can lead to your ad spend disappearing into a black hole, with little to show for it. Here's why budget optimization is crucial:

- **Efficiency Enhancer:** Optimizing your ad spend ensures you're not wasting money on irrelevant clicks or impressions. You'll reach the right audience and maximize the impact of your campaigns.
- **Data-Driven Decisions:** By tracking key metrics and analyzing campaign performance data, you can make informed decisions about where to allocate your budget for the best ROI.
- **Scaling for Success:** As you refine your targeting and optimize your campaigns, you can confidently scale your ad spend, reaching a wider audience and achieving your social media goals.

The Budget Balancing Act:

Optimizing your ad spend requires a strategic balancing act. Here are some key considerations:

- **Campaign Goals:** Clearly define your campaign goals (e.g., brand awareness, website traffic, lead generation, sales). This will guide your budget allocation decisions.
- **Target Audience:** Understanding your ideal customer and their online behavior is crucial for setting realistic budgets and reaching the right people.
- **Bidding Strategies:** Explore different bidding options offered by social media platforms, such as cost-per-click (CPC) or cost-per-thousand impressions (CPM), to optimize your budget based on your goals.
- **A/B Testing:** Continuously test different ad variations, targeting options, and budget allocations to see what delivers the best results.

The Tools of the Trade:

Here are some valuable tools available on most social media platforms to help you optimize your ad spend:

- **Campaign Budget Optimization:** Utilize built-in campaign budget optimization tools that automatically adjust your budget allocation across ad sets for maximum performance.

- **Conversion Tracking:** Set up conversion tracking to monitor how your ads are driving desired actions, such as website purchases or email signups. This data is essential for optimizing your budget for conversions.
- **Audience Insights:** Leverage audience insights tools to gain a deeper understanding of your target audience's demographics, interests, and online behavior. This can inform your budget allocation strategies.

The Budgeting Bonanza Boss:

By mastering the art of budget optimization, you'll transform yourself from a budgeting novice to a budgeting bonanza boss. Here's what you'll gain from this chapter:

- The importance of setting clear campaign goals to guide your ad spend
- Strategies for allocating your budget based on your target audience
- Techniques for leveraging different bidding options to optimize your budget
- Tips for using A/B testing to refine your budget allocation strategies

- Knowledge of valuable tools for tracking conversions and optimizing ad performance

Remember, effective social media advertising is not about throwing the most money at the problem. By following these strategies and using the available tools, you can become a budgeting bonanza boss, ensuring your social media ad spend delivers a maximum return on investment and fuels your long-term success.

Chapter 17: Tracking and Tweaking: Analyzing Data to Refine Your Paid Strategy

In the ever-evolving world of social media advertising, success hinges on your ability to learn and adapt. This chapter dives into the power of data analysis, equipping you with the knowledge and strategies to become a data-driven detective, uncovering valuable insights from your campaigns and using them to refine your paid social media strategy for continuous improvement.

The Data Deluge Dilemma:

Social media platforms generate a vast amount of data on your advertising campaigns. However, simply having data isn't enough. Here's why data analysis is crucial for success:

- **Uncover Hidden Gems:** Data analysis reveals valuable insights into how your ads are performing, what resonates with your audience, and where there's room for improvement.
- **Tweaking for Triumph:** By analyzing data, you can identify areas for optimization, such as refining your targeting parameters, A/B testing different ad creatives, or adjusting your budget allocation.
- **The Road to ROI:** Data analysis helps you measure your return on investment (ROI) and

ensure you're getting the most out of your ad spend.

The Data Detective's Toolkit:

Fortunately, most social media platforms offer a robust set of analytics tools to help you crack the data code. Here are some key metrics to track:

- **Impressions:** The number of times your ad was displayed.
- **Clicks:** The number of times users clicked on your ad.
- **Click-Through Rate (CTR):** The percentage of people who saw your ad and clicked on it. (Clicks divided by Impressions)
- **Conversions:** The number of desired actions taken, such as website purchases, lead signups, or app downloads.
- **Cost per Acquisition (CPA):** The average cost you incur for each conversion.

From Data to Decisions:

Here's how to transform raw data into actionable insights for optimizing your paid strategy:

- **Set SMART Goals:** Establish clear, Specific, Measurable, Achievable, Relevant, and Time-bound goals for your campaigns. This provides a benchmark for evaluating your data and measuring success.

- **Track Performance Regularly:** Don't wait until the end of the campaign to analyze your data. Monitor key metrics regularly to identify trends and make adjustments as needed.
- **Identify Winning Elements:** Analyze which ad variations, targeting options, or campaign elements are performing best. Replicate these winning elements in future campaigns.
- **Test and Refine Relentlessly:** Embrace a culture of continuous testing. Experiment with different strategies, analyze the results, and refine your approach based on the data you uncover.

The Data-Driven Maestro:

By mastering the art of data analysis, you'll transform yourself from a data novice to a data-driven maestro, conducting your paid social media strategy like a well-oiled machine. Here's what you'll gain from this chapter:

- The importance of setting SMART goals to guide your data analysis
- Knowledge of key metrics to track for measuring campaign performance

- Strategies for interpreting data and uncovering valuable insights
- Tips for using data to identify winning elements and replicate success
- Techniques for employing A/B testing and continuous refinement for ongoing improvement

Remember, data is the key to unlocking the true potential of your paid social media advertising. By becoming a data-driven detective and leveraging the power of analysis, you can continuously refine your strategy, optimize your campaigns for maximum impact, and achieve your social media advertising goals.

Chapter 18: Building Your Brand Voice: Finding Your Unique Tone and Style

In the crowded social media landscape, standing out from the noise requires a distinct brand voice. This chapter delves into the art of crafting a unique tone and style that resonates with your audience and embodies your brand identity.

The Voice of the Crowd Conundrum:

Many brands blend into the background with generic messaging. Here's why a distinct brand voice is crucial:

- **Memorable Magic:** A unique voice makes your brand memorable and helps you stand out from the competition.
- **Audience Affinity:** The right tone can connect with your audience on a deeper level, fostering trust and loyalty.
- **Brand Personality Power:** Your brand voice reflects your brand personality. It conveys your values, culture, and how you want to be perceived by your audience.

The Voice Vault: Unlocking Your Brand's Persona

Before crafting your voice, consider your brand's unique personality:

- **Brand Values:** Identify your core values and beliefs. What does your brand stand for?
- **Target Audience:** Who are you trying to reach? Understanding your audience's preferences and communication style is key.
- **Brand Personality Traits:** Imagine your brand as a person. What are their personality traits? Friendly, authoritative, humorous, or something else entirely?

From Persona to Voice:

Here's how to translate your brand persona into a distinct voice:

- **Formal or Informal?** Choose a level of formality that aligns with your brand personality and resonates with your audience.
- **Word Choice Wizardry:** Select words that reflect your brand's values and personality. Are you playful and lighthearted, or sophisticated and professional?
- **Conversational Cadence:** Develop a conversational style that feels natural and authentic for your brand. Imagine you're having a conversation with your ideal customer.
- **Emotional Intelligence:** Infuse your voice with the emotions you want to evoke in your

audience. Do you want to inspire, educate, entertain, or something else?

The Voice in Action:

Here are some practical tips for implementing your brand voice across your social media platforms:

- **Consistent is King (or Queen):** Maintain consistency in your voice across all platforms to create a unified brand experience.
- **Content Chameleon:** While your voice should remain consistent, adapt it slightly to suit different content formats (e.g., captions, videos, tweets).
- **Read it Out Loud:** Before hitting post, read your content aloud. Does it sound natural and authentic for your brand voice?

The Voice Virtuoso:

By following these strategies, you'll transform yourself from a voice impersonator to a voice virtuoso. Here's what you'll gain from this chapter:

- Techniques for identifying your brand's core values and personality
- Tips for selecting the right level of formality and word choice for your brand voice

- Strategies for developing a conversational style that feels natural and authentic
- Methods for infusing your voice with the emotions you want to evoke in your audience
- Ideas for maintaining brand voice consistency across all your social media platforms

Remember, your brand voice is a powerful tool for building relationships with your audience. By crafting a unique and compelling voice, you can make your brand stand out in the social media crowd and forge lasting connections with your customers.

Chapter 19: Influencer Outreach: Partnering with Powerhouses to Amplify Your Reach

In today's social media landscape, influencers wield significant power to shape brand perception and drive consumer decisions. This chapter equips you with the knowledge and strategies to navigate the world of influencer outreach, forming successful partnerships that amplify your brand reach and achieve your marketing goals.

The Influencer Influence:

Influencers have become a powerful marketing force for several reasons:

- **Trust and Authenticity:** Consumers often trust influencer recommendations more than traditional advertising, perceiving them as genuine and relatable.
- **Targeted Audience Access:** Influencers have built dedicated communities around their niche interests, granting you access to a highly targeted audience.
- **Content Creation Powerhouse:** Influencers are skilled content creators who can generate engaging content that resonates with their audience and promotes your brand in a natural way.

Beyond the Follower Count:

While follower count is a metric to consider, it shouldn't be the sole focus when choosing influencer partners. Here are key factors for successful influencer outreach:

- **Alignment with Brand Values:** Select influencers whose values and personality align with your brand identity to ensure an authentic partnership.
- **Audience Relevance:** Partner with influencers who have a target audience that overlaps with your ideal customer base.
- **Engagement Rate:** Look beyond follower count and prioritize influencers with a high engagement rate, indicating a more active and receptive audience.
- **Content Quality:** Choose influencers who create high-quality, engaging content that aligns with your brand's aesthetic and messaging.

The Art of the Influencer Ask:

Reaching out to influencers requires a strategic approach. Here are some tips for crafting a winning influencer outreach strategy:

- **Personalize Your Approach:** Avoid generic templates. Research the influencer and tailor your message to their specific interests and content style.

- **Value Proposition Powerhouse:** Clearly articulate the value proposition for the influencer. What's in it for them? Highlight potential benefits like brand exposure, product access, or an engaged audience.
- **Campaign Clarity:** Clearly outline your campaign goals, target audience, and the type of content you envision. This ensures alignment and avoids misunderstandings.
- **Respectful Negotiation:** Be professional and respectful in your communication. Negotiate terms fairly and be open to creative collaboration.

The Influencer Partnership Maestro:

By mastering the art of influencer outreach, you'll transform yourself from an influencer novice to an influencer partnership maestro. Here's what you'll gain from this chapter:

- Understanding of the power and influence that influencers hold in today's social media marketing landscape
- Knowledge of key factors to consider when selecting the right influencer partners for your brand

- Strategies for crafting personalized and compelling influencer outreach messages
- Tips for effectively communicating your campaign goals and value proposition to potential partners
- Techniques for negotiating mutually beneficial influencer partnerships

Remember, successful influencer marketing goes beyond simply throwing money at popular personalities. By building genuine partnerships with the right influencers, you can leverage their social clout to amplify your brand reach, engage a wider audience, and achieve your marketing objectives.

Chapter 20: Building Your Social Media Dream Team: Tools and Resources to Streamline Your Workflow

In today's fast-paced social media world, managing multiple platforms and creating engaging content can feel overwhelming. This chapter equips you with the knowledge and resources to assemble your social media dream team – a treasure trove of tools and platforms designed to streamline your workflow, boost your efficiency, and empower you to achieve social media success.

The One-Person Powerhouse Paradox:

Many social media managers try to do it all themselves, often leading to burnout and inefficiencies. Here's why leveraging the right tools is crucial:

- **Time Management Triumph:** Social media management tools help you schedule posts in advance, track performance metrics, and manage multiple platforms from a central hub, freeing up valuable time.
- **Content Creation Powerhouse:** Design tools, photo editors, and video editing platforms empower you to create high-quality, engaging content without needing a professional design team.

- **Data-Driven Decisions:** Analytics and reporting tools provide valuable insights into your audience engagement and campaign performance, allowing you to make data-driven decisions for continuous improvement.

The Social Media Management Symphony:

Here are some key categories of tools to consider for your social media dream team:

- **Social Media Management Platforms:** These platforms allow you to schedule posts, monitor conversations, and analyze performance across various social media networks. Popular options include Hootsuite, Buffer, and Sprout Social.
- **Content Creation Tools:** Canva, Adobe Spark, and Lumen5 are just a few of the many tools available to create stunning visuals, infographics, and even short videos without needing design expertise.
- **Analytics and Reporting Tools:** Built-in analytics from social media platforms and third-party tools like Google Analytics offer valuable insights into audience demographics, engagement metrics, and website traffic generated from your social media efforts.

Building Your Dream Team:

Here are some steps to take to assemble your social media dream team:

- **Identify Your Needs:** Audit your current workflow and identify areas where you can save time, improve efficiency, or gain deeper insights.
- **Research and Explore:** Research different social media management tools, content creation platforms, and analytics solutions to find the ones that best suit your needs and budget.
- **Free Trials and Demos:** Take advantage of free trials and demos offered by many platforms to test-drive the tools before committing.
- **Integrations for Efficiency:** Look for tools that integrate seamlessly with each other, allowing you to streamline your workflow and avoid data silos.

The Social Media Tech Titan:

By assembling your social media dream team, you'll transform yourself from a one-person social media team to a social media tech titan. Here's what you'll gain from this chapter:

- Knowledge of different categories of social media management tools available

- Tips for identifying your specific needs and selecting the right tools for your workflow
- Strategies for leveraging content creation platforms to produce high-quality content without design expertise
- Techniques for using analytics and reporting tools to measure your social media performance and make data-driven decisions
- Methods for integrating different tools to streamline your workflow and maximize efficiency

Remember, you don't have to go it alone in the social media world. By leveraging the power of the right tools and resources, you can build your social media dream team and achieve your social media goals with greater efficiency and effectiveness.

Chapter 21: The Metrics that Matter: Tracking Your Progress and Measuring Success

In the ever-evolving world of social media, success hinges on your ability to measure and analyze your efforts. This chapter equips you with the knowledge and strategies to become a metrics master, identifying the key performance indicators (KPIs) that truly matter and using them to track your progress, measure success, and optimize your social media strategy for continuous improvement.

The Measurement Maze:

Social media platforms generate a vast amount of data, but not all metrics are created equal. Here's why focusing on the right metrics is crucial:

- **Goal-Oriented Guidance:** Tracking the right metrics ensures your efforts are aligned with your overall social media goals, whether it's brand awareness, website traffic, lead generation, or sales.
- **Data-Driven Decisions:** Analyzing key metrics allows you to identify areas for improvement and make informed decisions about your social media content, targeting strategies, and budget allocation.
- **Demonstrating ROI:** Tracking and reporting on relevant metrics helps you demonstrate the

return on investment (ROI) of your social media efforts to stakeholders.

The Metrics Matchmaker:

The specific metrics you track will depend on your unique social media goals. Here's a breakdown of some common goals and their corresponding key metrics:

- **Brand Awareness:** Focus on metrics like impressions, reach, follower growth, and brand mentions.
- **Website Traffic:** Track website clicks, link clicks, and referral traffic generated from your social media activity.
- **Lead Generation:** Monitor lead form submissions, signups, and downloads of gated content triggered by your social media efforts.
- **Sales:** Track social media-driven conversions (purchases) through UTM parameters or social commerce features.
- **Engagement:** Analyze metrics like likes, comments, shares, saves, and replies to gauge how well your content resonates with your audience.

Beyond the Numbers:

While quantitative metrics are important, don't neglect qualitative factors. Here are some additional considerations:

- **Brand Sentiment:** Track brand mentions and sentiment analysis to understand how people perceive your brand on social media.
- **Customer Satisfaction:** Monitor social media for customer feedback and identify areas where you can improve customer service and brand experience.
- **Industry Benchmarks:** Compare your social media performance with industry benchmarks to understand your competitive standing.

The Metrics Mastermind:

By mastering the art of social media measurement, you'll transform yourself from a metrics novice to a metrics mastermind. Here's what you'll gain from this chapter:

- The importance of aligning your tracked metrics with your overall social media goals
- Knowledge of key metrics for measuring brand awareness, website traffic, lead generation, sales, and audience engagement
- Strategies for tracking both quantitative and qualitative metrics for a holistic view of your social media performance

- Tips for utilizing social media analytics tools and reports to gain valuable insights
- Techniques for comparing your performance against industry benchmarks to identify areas for improvement

Remember, data is only valuable if you use it to your advantage. By becoming a metrics master and tracking the right data points, you can gain a deep understanding of your social media performance, make data-driven decisions, and continuously optimize your strategy to achieve your social media goals.

Chapter 22: Staying Ahead of the Curve: Keeping Pace with Evolving Social Media Trends

The social media landscape is in a constant state of flux. New platforms emerge, features evolve, and user behavior shifts. This chapter equips you with the knowledge and strategies to become a social media trendsetter, staying ahead of the curve by identifying and embracing emerging trends to keep your audience engaged and your brand at the forefront.

The Trend Chaser's Trap:

Simply chasing every fleeting trend can be a recipe for disaster. Here's why understanding and strategically leveraging trends is crucial:

- **Relevance Reigns Supreme:** By capitalizing on relevant trends, you can create fresh, engaging content that resonates with your audience and positions your brand as innovative and forward-thinking.
- **Engagement Explosion:** Emerging trends often present exciting opportunities to connect with your audience in new ways, sparking conversation and boosting engagement.
- **Staying Competitive:** Keeping pace with evolving trends ensures your brand doesn't become outdated or irrelevant in the ever-changing social media landscape.

The Trend Spotting Toolkit:

Staying ahead of the curve requires proactive vigilance. Here are some tools and strategies to identify emerging social media trends:

- **Social Listening Tools:** Utilize social listening tools to track brand mentions, industry conversations, and trending hashtags to identify emerging topics and audience interests.
- **Industry Publications and Blogs:** Subscribe to industry publications and blogs focused on social media marketing to stay informed about the latest trends and best practices.
- **Social Media Platforms Themselves:** Pay close attention to platform announcements, algorithm updates, and new features introduced by social media platforms. These often signal upcoming trends.
- **Competitor Analysis:** Keep an eye on your competitors' social media strategies. See what they're doing and identify trends they're embracing that you can adapt for your own brand.

The Trend-Worthy Transformer:

Not all trends are created equal. Here's how to evaluate trends and determine if they're worth incorporating into your social media strategy:

- **Alignment with Brand Values:** Ensure the trend aligns with your brand identity and target audience. Don't jump on a bandwagon just because it's popular.
- **Content Creation Capabilities:** Consider your resources and ability to create high-quality content that capitalizes on the trend effectively.
- **Long-Term Potential:** Distinguish between fleeting fads and trends with staying power. Focus on trends that offer long-term engagement opportunities.

The Social Media Trendsetter:

By mastering the art of staying ahead of the curve, you'll transform yourself from a trend follower to a social media trendsetter. Here's what you'll gain from this chapter:

- Understanding of the importance of identifying and embracing emerging social media trends
- Knowledge of various tools and strategies for trend spotting and staying informed
- Techniques for evaluating trends and determining their relevance to your brand and audience
- Tips for strategically incorporating trends into your social media content to boost engagement

- Strategies for maintaining a forward-thinking and innovative social media presence

Remember, social media success is not about being stagnant. By staying ahead of the curve and embracing emerging trends, you can keep your audience engaged, your brand relevant, and your social media strategy future-proofed for ongoing success.

Part 6: Bonus Chapter: 27 Proven Hacks in 5 Minutes (For the Super Busy Marketer)

Short on time? Need some quick and easy wins to boost your social media game? This bonus chapter gives you 27 actionable hacks you can implement in just minutes to maximize your social media marketing impact.

Content Creation Hacks:

1. **Repurpose Existing Content:** Breathe new life into old blog posts or videos by creating social media snippets, infographics, or short threads.
2. **Leverage User-Generated Content:** Feature content created by your followers to boost engagement and authenticity.
3. **Schedule Social Media Posts in Advance:** Free up your time by batch-creating and scheduling content for the entire week.
4. **Curate Compelling Content:** Share valuable content from industry leaders to establish yourself as a thought leader.
5. **Embrace Visual Storytelling:** Use high-quality images and videos to grab attention and tell your brand story effectively.

Engagement Hacks:

6. **Ask Engaging Questions:** Spark conversation by posing thought-provoking questions relevant to your target audience.
7. **Run Interactive Polls and Quizzes:** Encourage audience participation with interactive elements that provide valuable insights.
8. **Respond to Comments and Messages Promptly:** Show your audience you care by responding to comments and messages in a timely manner.
9. **Run Social Media Contests and Giveaways:** Generate excitement and attract new followers with fun contests and giveaways.
10. **Host Live Q&A Sessions:** Connect with your audience in real-time through live video sessions.

Growth Hacks:

11. **Optimize Your Social Media Profiles:** Craft compelling bios, use relevant keywords, and include high-quality profile pictures and cover images.
12. **Utilize Relevant Hashtags:** Research and include targeted hashtags to increase your content's discoverability.
13. **Promote Your Social Media on Other Channels:** Drive traffic to your social media

profiles by promoting them on your website, email signature, and marketing materials.

14. **Collaborate with Influencers:** Partner with relevant influencers to reach a wider audience and leverage their credibility.

15. **Run Paid Social Media Ads:** Invest in targeted social media ads to reach a highly specific audience and achieve your marketing goals.

Time-Saving Hacks:

16. **Use Social Media Management Tools:** Streamline your workflow by utilizing scheduling platforms and analytics tools.

17. **Create Content Calendars:** Plan your content in advance to ensure consistent posting and avoid last-minute scrambles.

18. **Batch-Create Visuals:** Design a week's worth of social media graphics in one sitting to save time.

19. **Repurpose Content Across Platforms:** Tailor your content for different social media platforms to maximize its reach.

20. **Utilize Social Media Listening Tools:** Stay informed about brand mentions and industry conversations to identify potential opportunities.

Analytics Hacks:

21. **Track Key Performance Indicators (KPIs):** Focus on metrics that matter most to your social media goals (e.g., engagement, website traffic, leads).
22. **Analyze Your Audience Demographics:** Understand your audience's demographics and interests to tailor your content accordingly.
23. **Monitor Industry Benchmarks:** Compare your performance against industry averages to identify areas for improvement.
24. **Run A/B Tests:** Experiment with different content formats, posting times, and calls to action to see what resonates best with your audience.
25. **Regularly Review and Refine Your Strategy:** Social media is ever-evolving. Regularly assess your strategy and adapt based on data and new trends.

Brand Advocacy Hacks:

26. **Highlight Customer Testimonials and Reviews:** Showcase positive feedback from satisfied customers to build trust and credibility.
27. **Run Employee Advocacy Programs:** Encourage your employees to share your brand content and stories on their social media channels.

Remember, consistency is key! By implementing a few of these hacks each week, you can significantly improve your social media marketing efforts and achieve your social media goals, even on a tight schedule.

www.ingramcontent.com/pod-product-compliance
Lightning Source LLC
LaVergne TN
LVHW051739050326
832903LV00023B/1007